Shadow Man

Margaret Chula

A Publication of The Poetry Box®

©2019 Margaret Chula
All rights reserved.

Editing & book design by Shawn Aveningo Sanders.
Cover photo by D. Gupta.
Cover design by Shawn Aveningo Sanders.
Author photo by John Hall.

No part of this book may be reproduced in any manner whatsoever without permission from the author, except in the case of brief quotations embodied in critical essays, reviews and articles.

ISBN: 978-1-948461-45-0
Printed in the United States of America.

Published by The Poetry Box®, 2019
Beaverton, Oregon
ThePoetryBox.com

"Whatever is real, casts shadows."

Jane Hirshfield

"Shadows are light that is struck out."

Paul Chan, artist

Contents

Cracks	7
Shoes	9
A Letter to My Father	10
Upbeat	12
Breaking Even	13
Ninth Inning	14
Questions for My Sister	16
The Reunion	18
Unabashed Greed	20
The yellow house on Conway Street	22
Emperor Penguins	23
Visitation	25
Promises	27
What Was Lost	28
His death was soundless	30
In the Shadows	31
Eulogy	32
Acknowledgments	35
Praise for *Shadow Man*	37
About the Author	39
About The Poetry Box	41

Cracks

Lying on the couch
tipping back a Budweiser,
he notices
some hairline cracks
in the ceiling.

All day his eyes
have focused on bricks
and trowels and mortar
to hold a building together.

He smells the stale sweat
that has come to live
in his shirt collar,

listens to the rasp
of his breath,
coiled springs
detaching.

These stubby fingers
once held each
of his five children
offered in Baptism,

a dribble of holy water
marking a cross
of protection
on their foreheads.

Now his daughters
practice gymnastics
in the backyard
with no one
to spot them.

[. . .]

His sons play catch
with each other
while waiting
for a pitcher.

His wife locks him out
on nights when he
binges with the boys.

Tomorrow
he will take out the ladder
and fix those cracks
in the ceiling
before the roof
caves in
on them all.

Shoes

after a photograph by Tracy Paul Pitts

On the day of my First Communion, I'm standing
on the sidewalk in front of St. Patrick's Church

in a white lace dress and veil waiting for Daddy
who dropped me off and promised to come back.

The other fathers are dressed in suits and ties,
their shoes so shiny I can lean over and see my reflection.

My father wears work boots with soles so thick
they can walk over nails, screws, and latches—

things that hold his life together. Like his tin
lunch pail that keeps his bologna and mayonnaise

sandwich fresh until the noon bell sounds
and he and his pals sit on picnic benches

to eat their lunches and smoke Camels
before putting on their crusty work gloves.

My gloves are in my pocket to keep them clean
for my First Communion—white as

my new Mary Janes, shoes with buckles,
not shoelaces that can come untied.

The other fathers are holding
their daughters' hands and laughing.

It's starting to get cold. I curl up my fingers
and watch the ants take over the sidewalk.

A Letter to My Father

> *When you were young, you needed something you did not receive, and you will never receive it. And the proper attitude is mourning—not blame—but mourning.*
>
> Alice Miller

What did you want me, your first-born daughter, to be?

The answer comes in a series of flashbacks, like photographs labeled "Daddy's Little Girl"—ribbons braided in my hair, dresses with crinoline petticoats that I twirled around ever so gracefully for your pleasure, reciting nursery rhymes I'd learned in school, serving you tea in dollhouse cups.

But the pretty little girl fades as I remember first grade and being scolded by Mrs. North for playing with trucks on the boys' side. And that Friday night shopping trip to the A&P when our car was stolen and, with it, my blankie. I cried for my blankie and for my cat, Pickles, run over by a car. And then I gave up trucks and baby blankets and cats—things that could be taken away from me.

When you built Kathy and me a crib for our dolls, I dutifully filled it. But what I really wanted was to learn how to *make* a crib. Later I coveted David's wood-burning kit, the pungent smell as drill bored through cedar. I would rather soar on my swing than dress paper dolls—explore lands beyond our house. When the boys banned me from their clubhouse, I borrowed your tools and built my own. Instead of flowers, I collected Popsicle sticks to make cities in the sand.

Did you ever stop to notice what I wanted? Did you see the skinned knees beneath my First Communion dress? Or just your virtuous daughter who would marry a nice Catholic boy, a church wedding with Aunt Jenny singing in the choir as I waltzed up the aisle on your arm. You, the proud father giving me away.

But there was no church wedding, no fancy bridal gown, and you were not there to give me away because I was not yours to give away. I chose a husband who has traveled around the world, but who could not tell you who won the World Series. And I produced no grandchildren for you to build cribs for or teach how to hit a fastball.

Every year I send you photographs of myself trekking in the Himalayas, sailing in Tahiti, exploring the jungles of Sarawak. And every time I visit, you open your wallet and show me the faded photograph of a nine-year-old girl in a pink dress smiling up at her Daddy.

Upbeat

after James Tate

The cat curls up in the corner
kneading its claws into the wallpaper.
It's a cold day, but sunbeams
occasionally break through the clouds.
The cat licks its fur and yawns and purrs.
Every now and then, it flicks its tail.
At dawn, when everyone is sleeping,
it jumps up on the piano bench
and plays Scott Joplin tunes.
This is how I cheer myself up
the young girl explains
to her deadbeat dad.

Breaking Even

Looking for Daddy
at the greyhound race track—
so many fat old men
emerge from the stadium
blinking in the sunlight.

How did you find me?
he asks studying the list
for Race #10.
TV monitors flicker.
I count the bruises on his legs.

What's your lucky number?
Four, I say. It means
"death" in Japanese.
He rises to place our bets
unshaven face, unsteady gait.

Are you having fun, dear?
he asks after two hours
of steady losses.
From the smoke-filled room,
we watch the muzzled greyhounds.

In the parking lot
he says, *You brought me luck
winning that last race!*
And another visit ends
just breaking even.

Ninth Inning

In fifth grade, Mrs. Forbes displays the girl's
illustrated book reports on the bulletin board.
You're going to be a children's book artist, she says.

She hit a home run and didn't even know
she was playing the game.

Her father hits a lot of home runs.
Handsome in his Greenfield All Stars uniform,
he pitches no-hit innings against the local teams.

She's more of a bench sitter, second string,
the only one in her class with divorced parents.
Always in left field when it comes to fun and games.

Her father turns down an agent's offer to play
in the semi-pros. "Stud" is content to play
it safe, hanging out with his hometown pals.

She wants to be an artist, but takes stenography
in high school so she can get a job. Always
a loyal team member, she transcribes

her boss's 110-word–a-minute dictation
into perfectly typed letters to impress his clients
and to pay her rent on a Beacon Street walk-up.

She loves the precision of shorthand. So much
like her father's spin ball—the beauty of lines
and curves that only they can appreciate.

Her father strikes out in the ninth inning.
No wife, no kids or grandchildren—not even a pet
he dies alone in the back of an ambulance.

Who can predict how the game will end?

Today is the first day of spring training.
The girl begins to write down her own words
as if her life depended on it.

Questions for My Sister

Remember going to the Northfield Drive-In on Friday nights? You and I in our Cinderella pajamas, Mother and Daddy in the front seat of the '56 Plymouth, the baby on Mother's lap. Even at age seven, you were mortified when Daddy made David and Stephen climb into the trunk before we got to the ticket booth.

We parked near the back so no one would see them scramble out of the trunk and join us in the back seat. They were just five and three, and we knew they'd fall asleep right after the cartoons.

Daddy rolled down the window and hooked up the speaker. He was the only one who knew how to attach it so it would stay on. Mother had popped popcorn that afternoon—holding the baby in one arm, turning the handle of the popcorn maker with the other. We watched her drizzle the butter. Sometimes she let us sprinkle on the salt. Then Daddy would take over, tossing the popped corn into the air. They always landed in the yellow bowl—not one kernel on the counter.

At the Drive-In, Mother divided the popcorn into our plastic cereal bowls and poured cherry Zarex into Dixie cups. Just in time for Woody Woodpecker, the first cartoon. I loved this wacky bird and his insane stutter. Remember how we'd mimic him in the back seat until Mother said *Shush! Enough!* I loved Donald and Daisy Duck, too, but hated Mickey and Minnie because they reminded me of mice in the pantry. Daddy prying their crushed bodies out of steel traps.

Remember how Daddy laughed at all the cartoons—how Mother didn't? How we tried to stay awake for the love scenes with Mitzi Gaynor and Rock Hudson? And the way Mother leaned closer to Daddy, his arm draped gently around her shoulder so as not to wake the baby. And later, how he carried us up to our beds, one by one, on those hot New England nights, bright stars filling the sky.

And I'm sure you remember that cold February morning when Mother packed us five kids into the car. There were no stars shining as she drove away, leaving Daddy behind.

The Reunion

Turners Falls, Massachusetts, 1986

After eight years and twenty countries,
the road ends in a New England mill town
outside your door. Late November,
the season of remembering.

You take a long time to answer.
I wait, stiffly grown-up, a woman
with broad shoulders and fair hair.
You, a fat man in a bathrobe,
embrace your first born,
as tall as you now.

Are you the man who tightened my ice skates
whose baseball pictures I kept framed on my dresser
who built me a swing so I could fly?
Why was it so easy, then, to sweep you
into the dustbin with the pressed butterflies
and paper dolls of childhood?

I sit on your bed, a ten-year-old swinging
between past and present. You call me
Margaret, not knowing me through years
of nicknames. Our silences are filled
with the blare of baseball games.

Out come the presents: pens and a calculator
scooped up from the campus where you work.
You, an old crow, carrying back shiny objects
to your nest. Most of the pens don't work.

You return to your baseball games that I have
interrupted—familiar hands resting in your lap

like roots of a great oak tree. There is still dirt
under your fingernails.

Photographs of your five children
are curling in the mirror, veiled
in a layer of dust. I can tell exactly
when each of us chose to desert you.

It's too late now. I have done without a father
for too many years and we don't have enough
in common to be friends.

I'm leaving you, too, as soon as I find the right door.
All those doors in my dreams that I never dared open,
I open now and stumble down the stairs into sunlight
leaving you framed in the doorway, in the dingy hallway
smelling of other people's cooking.

Unabashed Greed

Lust for oranges and peaches,
fruits with skins that peel off easily.
My hunger for the sweet juices of sweat
and sex, the taste of want and receive.

That inexplicable desire to swallow
warm milk from a cow's teats
or from my grandmother's, which
are dry and yet, I long for that touch.

I'm dying to sing every tune Joni Mitchell
sang, but even more tenderly. I want
her blond hair, too, to braid into wishes—
not three as in a fairytale, but unlimited

like stars that I pluck from the sky and run
my fingers along—those sharp points of light.
And why not go for Enlightenment—
giving up what I have, and replacing it

with something better. Like a new father
with soft hands to stroke my cheek. One
who offers me carnations instead of cigarettes.
We'd sip on martinis—not guzzle Budweisers

and afterwards, drive through the countryside—
me sitting next to him wearing butterflies
in my hair, him dapper in a white fedora.
And we'd take our time, as if there were

no clocks or wives or mothers to call us
to supper. Dinner, we'd call it, feasting
on squab, not kielbasa, and our rings
would glitter and clink against our glasses

as we toasted to the red convertible
and the hand-made Valentine
and to everything I once lacked
and now had.

The yellow house on Conway Street

is no longer yellow, the color of sunshine,
of five towheaded children spinning marbles
into a mud hole. Someone has painted it
the gray of elephant's breath, of dust kiddies,
or the acrid smoke of Daddy's Camels. The porch
is still there and the steps I hid beneath in the dirt
that smelled of fear as I listened to Mother and Daddy
argue before he left for work in the olive green Plymouth.

No sign of us anywhere. No walnut tree or the nuts
we hoarded in the pantry for winter. No hydrangeas
to make "hamburgers" with and sell on the sidewalk.
Not even a swing in the backyard.

> gnarled tree root
> cracks open the sidewalk
> *Pop Goes the Weasel!*

Emperor Penguins

One pale egg
in the female's pouch.
Carefully
she transfers it
to the male,
then marches
back to the sea.

The male penguin
stands
day and night
cradling the egg
in a pouch
between his legs.

Three months without food
in wind snow and ice,
sentinel
in a black
overcoat.

Frozen
in a fugue state,
he fuses his warmth
into the tiny embryo
incubating beneath
his feathers.

And when the chick
emerges
from its shell,
the father
weak from starvation

[. . .]

regurgitates
bits of his stomach lining
to feed the newborn.

How many nights
did we wait for Daddy
to come home
from his poker game
reeking of cigarettes
and beer?

Where was he
when I was lost
in the woods
with the boys
after dark?

After he died,
I took his overcoat
from the closet,
slipped my arms
into its silk-lined
sleeves

and wrapped it
around my body
as if it was a cloak
of warm
black
feathers.

Visitation

Krakow, 2003

I never expected to meet you here
in your motherland
but here you are
on *ul. Pilsudskiego*
fifty years old again
your pate just beginning to bald
webs of pain canting
shadows onto your face.
You're wearing the overcoat
that I knew as a child, grey tweed
mid-thigh—I swear I can smell
Mennen aftershave in your wake.

Is this how the dead come back
thousands of miles from where
you laid them to rest? Are you
here to find your parents
in this war-torn city?

What is it that you want to tell me?
Have you appeared with the full moon
on my birthday to remind me how Polish I am?
As if I don't already know—draped in scarves
and velvets with rings of amber, blond hair
streaming down my back—Saint Margaret
unrestrained. Like my forebears, I take refuge
in dark places to drink mead, covet sweets
that melt in my hands. Like them, I weep
over poetry, gravitate towards bones
and Madonnas, and stained glass martyrs.

[. . .]

Yes, Daddy, I am Polish, but I no longer believe
in heaven or resurrection or the Holy Ghost—
just an ordinary ghost walking down
a cobblestone street at dusk, broad back
moving steadily away from me
before I am tempted to follow.

Promises

made and broken, like pottery
not long enough in the kiln
    half-baked intentions gone awry
    a homing pigeon misguided by greed
    those kernels of cracked corn
    abandoned in winter dusk.

When I promised to bury you
I did not know you would die in winter
    ground frozen as the faces
    of your estranged children
    eulogy stuck in my throat
    mute red tongues of the poinsettia.

You did not make me promise
to remember you or to love you
and, for that reason, we stay connected
    like strings of flesh inside a squash
    wrapped around its seeds
    pale and moist
    and full of promise.

What Was Lost

I wanted so much from him: a swing, a wood burning kit,
a blue prom dress. I wanted him to give me money
for school lunches instead of having to dig for loose
change fallen between the couch cushions.

I prayed that he would come to my graduation, my
farewell party, and later my marriage in a courthouse.
I guess he was tired of courthouses and jails and begging
to see his children who had been turned against him.

I wanted one of his red plaid hunting shirts for the stale
tobacco smell of him, wanted to rub the rough wool
against my cheek and imagine his whiskers before
he shaved, and his soft cheeks afterwards.

When I saw him last, he was breathing oxygen
from a tube that he carried around his apartment
like a limp garden hose.

We sat on the sofa and he took out a box of treasures:
newspaper clippings; my letters from Japan; a photo
of him as a child; his marriage certificate; and a stack
of old receipts.

*I want you to know that I gave money to your mother
for you kids. It wasn't much, but I did the best I could.*

I thought I had lost them, but today I found those musty
proofs of child support from the Probation Office
of the District Court of Franklin County. Twenty dollars,
thirty, forty—more than three hundred checks
during those twelve years.

On the other side of the country, I am sitting on the sofa in my sunlit room arranging the receipts by date, giving order to sorrow—my father's final gift to me, bound up tightly with twine.

His death was soundless

no guttural cry
to complete the circle,
nor pitiful whimper.
No last words of futility
and complaints that fill
the days of the dying.

His embalmed face issued
no expression, but I could hear
that desolate voice
that called me, year after year,
across the country to his doorstep,
to the sound of his gout-footed limp
and the latch being released
and my name being called
the way no other has said it.

I stood by his open coffin
at Kostanski's Funeral Home,
no baseball games to conceal
our silence. Outside, icicles
melted in the early winter sun.
My tears dripped onto his face.

He could not speak,
nor could I—
father and daughter
from beginning to end
forever holding our peace.

In the Shadows

a tanka sequence

Refrigerated for days
my father waits for me
to lay him to rest
in the cemetery
of the Sorrowful Mother.

My strong father
helpless now in his new suit
and perfectly knotted tie
    hands clenched around a white rose
    coffin filled with regrets.

I bury him
on the winter solstice
when shadows move toward light.
    How bright the red poinsettia—
    how black the crows.

Forty-nine days
after my father's death
the ground hog comes up
sees his own shadow
and returns underground.

Those wildflower seeds
embedded in the paper
of a sympathy card.
    I tear them into strips
    and plant them in the shadows.

Eulogy

For Stanley M. Chula, December 21, 2001

Today is the Winter Solstice, the shortest day of the year
and the longest night. Today the sun is at its lowest.
In ancient times, people brought out candles
to symbolize the return of sunlight.

Today, on this day of darkness, we gather to acknowledge
the life and death of Stanley Chula: father, grandfather,
partner, brother, uncle, and friend.

My father was a quiet man, a man of few words and strong
feelings. He loved his five children and his partner, Vickie.
It would have made him so happy to see you all here today.

He loved flowers and birds and took a walk nearly every day,
bringing back wildflowers and sometimes not-so-wild-flowers
that he had picked from the neighbors' yards.

He was not an educated man, but was skillful with his hands.
He built things with ease and pleasure. I remember the dolls'
crib he constructed for my sister and me from scraps of wood.
And the chairs and tables he rescued from the dump
and brought back to life.

He was a hard worker, gained satisfaction from a job well done.
For many years he worked at the Greenfield Tap & Die and then
on the construction crew at Deerfield Academy. When he retired,
he got a part-time job as a crossing guard at the Ryan Road School.
He enjoyed being with the children and they gave him Valentine
cards and presents.

My father was an outstanding athlete. He played All-Star
baseball in high school and semi-pro as a pitcher

on the Greenfield Tap & Die team. I remember him
teaching us how to throw a ball at a young age
and how to ice skate.

But most of all, I'm impressed with the simplicity of his life.
His pleasures in his old age were walking, watching sports TV
on playing bingo, going to the Hinsdale racetrack, and eating
breakfast every morning at the Blue Bonnet diner.

In this consumer-oriented society, he had few possessions.
His keepsakes were stored in a small wooden box that he'd made
by hand: photographs of his children; newspaper articles;
military mementos; cards, letters, and obituaries of his family.

My father did not like to buy things when he could repair them.
A few years ago, when I asked him what preparations
I should make for when he died, he said,
Just put me in a box and bury me in the ground.

And so today on the Winter Solstice, the turning point
between life and death and new life, when the light
begins to grow stronger and brighter
and we move steadily toward spring,
we put Stanley, Daddy,
into his box and lay him to rest.
May he find the light.

Acknowledgments

"Breaking Even," *Always Filling, Always Full* (White Pine Press, 2001)

"His death was soundless" received an Honorable Mention in the Oregon State Poetry Association Contest (2011)

"In the Shadows" was awarded First Prize in the Oregon State Poetry Association Contest (2006) and appeared in *Verseweavers*

"Ninth Inning," *The Poeming Pigeon: Sports* (The Poetry Box, 2019)

"Shoes" is an ekphrastic response to a photograph by Tracy Pitts featured in his solo show *We've Never Met, But I Think About You All the Time* at the Erickson Gallery, Portland, Oregon (2017)

"The yellow house on Conway Street," *Frogpond* (Fall 2012)

"Unabashed Greed," *bosque 7* (Bosque Press, 2017)

"Visitation," *Colere* (2013)

"What Was Lost" is forthcoming in *Show Us Your Papers* (Main Street Rag Press, 2020)

Many thanks to the talented and insightful women in my poetry groups: Cathy Cain, Christine Delea, Cindy Williams Gutiérrez, Diane Holland, Andrea Hollander, Carolyn Martin, Pattie Palmer-Baker, Paulann Petersen, Donna Prinzmetal, Joanna Rose, Shawn Aveningo Sanders, Penelope Scambly Schott, Suzanne Sigafoos, and Dianne Stepp.

Special thanks to Penelope Scambly Schott who said "I'm a sucker for father poems" and offered to read the manuscript. And, as always, to John Hall, my beloved husband and editor.

Kudos to Shawn Aveningo Sanders and Robert Sanders for their diligence, attention, and expertise in producing aesthetically beautiful books for The Poetry Box. It's been a pleasure working with them.

Praise for Shadow Man

"I wanted so much from you," writes the poet. The estranged father plays semi-pro ball, swigs beer, wears thick work boots, doesn't show up for his daughter's First Communion. "The other fathers are holding / their daughters' hands . . . I curl up my fingers / and watch the ants take over the sidewalk." *Shadow Man* is a deeply touching portrayal of love, loss, and forgiveness.

Penelope Scambly Schott
Oregon Book Award for Poetry

In her new collection, *Shadow Man*, Margaret Chula writes about poignant, often painful, memories of her father. She provides rich details of both his physical presence, from his aftershave to his workingman's shoes, and the many ways his lack of understanding affected her emotionally. Through Chula's insights, we as readers can understand our own fraught relationships with parents. As adults facing honest memory, we can arrive at the grace of reconciliation that she shows is possible and essential for our own serenity.

Bill Siverly, author of *Nightfall*

About the Author

 Margaret Chula has been writing, teaching, and publishing poetry for over forty years. Her books include: *Grinding my ink*; *Shadow Lines* (linked haibun with Rich Youmans); *Always Filling, Always Full*; *This Moment*; *The Smell of Rust*; *What Remains: Japanese Americans in Internment Camps* (with quilt artist Cathy Erickson); *Just This*; *Winter Deepens*; *Daffodils at Twilight*; and *One Leaf Detaches*. Grants from the Oregon Arts Commission and the Regional Arts and Culture Council have supported her work, as well as fellowships to the Vermont Studio Center, the Helene Wurlitzer Foundation, and Playa at Summer Lake.

Maggie has been a featured speaker and workshop leader at conferences throughout the United States, as well as in Poland, Canada, Peru, and Japan. She has also served as president of the Tanka Society of America and as Poet Laureate for Friends of Chamber Music. Living in Kyoto for twelve years, she now makes her home in Portland, Oregon, where she hikes, swims, and creates flower arrangements for every room of the house.

<www.margaretchula.com>

About The Poetry Box

The Poetry Box® was founded by Shawn Aveningo Sanders & Robert Sanders, who wholeheartedly believe that every day spent with the people you love, doing what you love, is a moment in life worth cherishing. Their boutique press celebrates the talents of their fellow artisans and writers through professional book design and publishing of individual collections, as well as their flagship literary journal, *The Poeming Pigeon*.

Feel free to visit the online bookstore (thePoetryBox.com), where you'll find more titles including:

November Quilt by Penelope Scambly Schott

Shrinking Bones by Judy K. Mosher

Epicurean Ecstasy by Cynthia Gallaher

The Poet's Curse by Michael Estabrook

Like the O in Hope by Jeanne Julian

The Unknowable Mystery of Other People by Sally Zakariya

Impossible Ledges by Dianne Avey

Painting the Heart Open by Liz Nakazawa

Bee Dance by Cathy Cain

Abruptio by Melissa Fournier

and more . . .

www.ingramcontent.com/pod-product-compliance
Lightning Source LLC
LaVergne TN
LVHW090040080526
838202LV00046B/3900